To my parents, family and my tribe, who came running to scrub dishes, set tables, haul trash, clean toilets, pick me up, and help me put one foot in front of the other. I'm eternally grateful.

And to you Peanut, Big, and Strong, and Smart, and Kind.

xoxoxo

TABLE OF CONTENTS

INTRODUCTION

1 SEE YOURSELF

2 RECOGNIZING YOUR FEAR

3 THE THING ABOUT RESPONSIBILITY

4 FANTASTY VS. REALITY

5 WHAT'S THE WORST THING THAT CAN HAPPEN

6 GET OUT

7 KENNYISMS

8 BACK TO YOUR FUTURE

9 I AM THE PARENT

10 MOVING ON

Disclaimer: This isn't a book that speaks in the language of therapy. The words codependency, enabling, and others that used to rightfully describe traits and experiences of loving an addict. They are true, and needed, and justified, but I am not a therapist nor am I an expert on the psychology behind toxic relationships, I'm just a woman who survived.

Introduction

Stop. No really, you just cracked open these fresh pages of this book and you need to stop. I want you to take a good long minute because what in the actual sweet baby Jesus is happening right now? I'm going to assume you picked this book of all the zillions of books to read because you are going through a chapter in your life that has you feeling like you got ran over by the trash truck, twice, while wearing your favorite dress. You know the dress that makes you feel like Julia Roberts in Pretty Woman, but the Opera Dress, not the street corner one. I'm also going to assume that as you read these very words you are trying with every single breath you take today to find your way back to standing upright, back to smiling, back to living.

So, before we run off down a much needed road together to talk about what action you need to take in order to see change in your life or what specific things will help you reclaim your life, we are going to take a hot minute to scream.

Yes. Scream.

I know, I know. It's not at all how you expected this book to begin. Books begin with soft wisdom where you, the reader, consume what I, the author, have passionately prepared for you, and you do so quietly, in private, in your head. I also know that screaming isn't what upstanding, reasonable, commonsense people do. Those people wouldn't dare scream at the top of their lungs. They wouldn't dare take every single overwhelming and irrational feeling they have and project them, loudly, to the outside world. Oh no, no way. We've been told over and over again that in our worst moments, in the darkest of our days, when we are scared, hurt, or completely flattened by the swirling chaos around us that we calmly and respectfully keep that shit show to ourselves never dreaming of bothering someone else with it. At the very least we should find a way to manage our emotions and process them in a "normal" way. Who decided what normal even was?!

Well guess what my friend, things are different here. This time we have together, these words on this page, this moment right here…this gives you permission to lose your ever living mind with anger, with grief, with sadness, with fear.

This is our time to be as real and as raw as we need to be to hold space for whatever negative and frankly dramatic thing you may feel about what you are going through. I certainly won't be the one to step in and judge you, because I've been there. I've been in those shoes you are wearing and I know those feelings all too well. We are going to dive into some pretty hard stuff on every page going forward, with each word intended to help you create the way out of the place you are in today. But, and that's a very large but…it's nearly impossible for the work to be done to move yourself forward if we can't first pause in acknowledgement that it is wholly and completely unfair, wildly awful, and down right maddening that you
are even here reading this damn book to begin with. My dear, it is the fucking worst, and it's 100% fine for you to scream about it if the good Lord moves you to, and on top of that, you don't owe anyone an apology for it. Not one single person. Because let's face it, I'm willing to bet you couldn't be more annoyed with people apologizing. I know I am.

When my ex-husband had spent the previous day rinking and was walking around like a puppy with his tail between his legs, he would apologize. When he had gotten yet another DUI, out would come an apology.

When we had gotten into a world ending top of our lungs shouting match where I would beg him to get help and he would ensure every weakness I've ever had was exploited, the apology would follow like clock work. And after my world collapsed looking like the bomb going off in Hiroshima, everyone around me had nothing to say except an apology. This isn't to say remorse, asking for forgiveness, and sympathy shouldn't exist, it absolutely should and needs to exist, but in this space, in this time, the necessity of your apology to create the perception that everything is fine and to ensure others feel comfortable around you is neither healthy nor required. Right now, in this single moment, there are thousands of emotions to be had, and not a single one has a need to be handled with refinement.

So, together, we can firmly say, this is the worst. The absolute, most insanely unimaginable, worst. In fact, while the iron is hot, let's go ahead and level up and openly speak about how truly terrifying this all is, and how hard even getting out bed feels, and how we've prayed with everything we have that it wouldn't happen, and most of all allow ourselves to feel completely overcome with the disappointment and unfairness of it all. That one right there, that big yet vastly unspoken emotion…disappointment. It often is stepped on by the more outwardly ugly and irrational emotions like anger and sadness that consume us in the moment, but disappointment…this hits right at the heart of it all. At the very foundation of your raw emotional truth, someone has failed to live up to the expectations that you crafted deep down in your heart for your life. Here in this moment, if you can give yourself permission to get loud, to forget politeness, and if you can sit with this for what it really is instead of pretending that you are strong enough to hold on to all these emotions, you will be able to overcome this Mt. Everest and move forward. Right now, today, if your deepest desire as you hold these words in your hands, is to pick up the pieces of your life and create a new future then it's time to be honest about what's going on, even if the only person listening is you. As if you need another reminder, here I am to bring up the topic of a global pandemic nobody saw coming. (Right?!) Today, we are all living in a world where every single human on the planet has a reason to feel disappointed. Yes, in varying degrees and, yes, each with different severity, but nonetheless since the pandemic began, simultaneously, each one of us regardless of location, age, race, gender, or privilege, has had a reason to hold grief, worry, and most of all disappointment all at the same time. And yet somehow in the midst of one of the most globally connected times in history, we humans also found ourselves in the thick of what

I will call woe is me comparison that left most of us feeling as if our problems, our worries, our situations were less than. A seemingly insurmountable human flaw, comparison, is working to steal away each of our unique versions of our life experiences. Listen to me right now, your worry, your fear, your disappointment is not less than, it is not meaningless, it is not insignificant. It is yours. And as painful as it may be, you my friend get to own it.

Have you ever attended a conference for work? Stay with me here, I promise we're going somewhere and that this will ultimately present an "ohhh I see" moment. Imagine you've just stepped off the airplane, in the dazzling, and sometimes dirty (as in actual dirt and often otherwise) all star hospitality city of Las Vegas. The instant you hit the terminal the music of slot machines rings through the air. Flashing, spinning, whirling, and blinking lights surround every inch of this place. The energy is, well, different here. Three thousand of your colleagues from around the globe have descended upon this city, ready to learn, network, invest in, and grow both themselves and their companies. It is the holy week for this group of professionals.

The hallways of the conference area filled shoulder to shoulder, casual conversation spills into catty gossip with the ever shifting tide of the newcomers and the veterans. This year though, something is different, something is brewing like that pot of coffee you turned on when you got up this morning but forgot about because the kids wouldn't get out of bed and you had to threaten all out war to get their sweet little faces up and out of the house before the school bus left them for you to deal with. Quiet whispers in the back of classrooms build to full blown lunch table conversations and soon, the entire conference is taken by a news story pouring in on every media platform from every corner of the globe. Pop up classes join the schedule every hour, and completely scrapped session plans all happen in a whirlwind. COVID-19 has arrived. At first, the coasters (the companies on the east and west coasts) took the lead. You are surrounded by the best hospitality companies, caterers, event planners, hotels, restaurants…and no one has any idea what's really coming. The camps of thought were tangible. There were those who made the choice to close down their business while away at conferences. (Margo, I'll never forget your foresight, strength, bravery, and leadership.) There are those who, like me, chose to watch closely, watch cautiously, but dredge forward into the darkness. The halls thin as the few days slip away. A historically bustling trade show floor is filled with timid vendors huddling in small groups in their collective dismay, all trying their best to salvage any hope of a sale to just ensure the booth they are standing in has a chance of being paid off. There is an unknown heaviness no one can explain yet everyone knows is present. An elephant in the room becomes the whole damn herd. And then, it comes like waves thrashing an unknown shore. The buzzing of constant calls. The ding of new emails pouring in. The chimes of texts. Clients are looking for guidance, seeking answers that don't exist, and more and more are using the words postpone and cancel. In an overnight shift of the cosmos, the world stopped and fear crept into the conference halls like the monsters under our beds as children, except this time even when you turned on the lights, they were there waiting for you. For some, it was instant, business was wiped out before anyone could gather their belongings and fly home. For others it will be weeks. Some lose their family business completely, closing their doors after 40 years. Some lose their jobs that they'd given countless hours of their lives to. Some find a way to pivot and hang on. Side note, can we all agree unless you are Ross Geller, you can never use the word pivot again?

And some, in the most horrific impact imaginable, are no longer living. One thing was universally true, for each one of the thousands that came to the twinkling lights of Las Vegas, each one felt the bitter sting of disappointment and no matter how the pandemic impacted their individual lives, some undeniably bigger than others, that didn't take away their unique right to feel it themselves. No matter the impact, no matter the level of devastation and destruction, no one could take away the fact that this happened, to all of us, and we had a very real reason to feel the tidal wave of emotions that continued (and hell, continue today) to crash in. Yes, we can see others' pain for their own, but that doesn't make our own any less important. Insert your "Ooooh I see."

Your disappointment is not petty nor small, no matter what others are going through at the same time. It matters. I'd like you to do something it took me far too many years to do. I want you to admit to yourself, right now, as you take these words in, the truth about what you are feeling about whatever situation you are in, whatever decision you are facing, whatever you are going through. I'd like you to shout it, scream it, cry it out, even if the emotions don't feel well-mannered.

You are a human being, going through something big, something life changing, something hard, and last time I checked you are not a SuperHero with some kind of infinite comic power that removes these challenges. Stop trying to hold on to your emotions, stop trying to reign them in. They are real and hear me right now…they are okay to feel.

So, now that we've stood face to face with the mirror of our emotions and recognized disappointment, sadness, fear, anger, what do we do? Do we stay here looking at this version of ourselves forever? No. Oh no my friend, we are never stuck but, although there are times that call for stillness. There have been many imes in my life that I've done everything in my power to move as quickly as humanly possible by a moment like this one.

I've crafted my way around some of the hardest, most excruciating experiences, sometimes without many noticing, and many times choosing to believe no one noticed even when I'm sure even the postal worker knew what was really going on. I would dive into another project, create something flashy and new. Diversion at its very finest. But now. Now I know better. Now, I know when to be still and allow myself to see things for what they are, not what I hope they are.

On our very first date, my ex told me he had just gotten out of prison. Our first date ya'll. I had known this person for less than one week. He was 19 years old and I was newly 21, you know the age of complete stupidity where you are old enough to be called an adult and do all the adult things but young enough that you shouldn't be allowed to make life long decisions. Yes, that age. I remember him telling me this while we were sitting in my tan Honda Accord, Rhoadie as she was very affectionately called, at a stop light next to a grocery store at 1:00am. He said it with a sense of timidness and yet held such clarity. I didn't say a word for a solid minute. Those were some intensely awkward seconds ticking by on the glowing red dash clock. What was swimming in my head was much louder. "Okay. Ooookaaaay. That's no big deal. He's clearly a good person and I'm obviously not an idiot so we are just going to move right past that and never tell anyone, ever.

Especially my former police officer father." When I finally realized I was going to have to respond, I fumbled through words that ensured it appeared I wasn't judging this person sitting in my car with me and that there was no way his admission would interfere with any chance of this possible relationship going past this date.

I didn't ask a single other question about the subject for months and we moved in together weeks later.

I didn't see things for what they were until now.

"Fire Hors D'oeuvres" I called over the radio as guests started to arrive high atop the city for a corporate event being held by one of my favorite clients. We had worked together several times over the past two years and I'd spent hours on building this professional relationship that now permitted me to leave her event early with her full trust that all would go as planned. I was almost 9 months pregnant and well, this walrus of a human needed to get off her feet. Something felt different and as I hugged her good-bye, I made the decision to call my doctor on the way home. I met my OB at her office shortly after I left the event where she assured me I had several more weeks before my baby would be making her grand entry into the world so I went home and did what any self respecting pregnant woman would do. I ate dessert and plopped down on the couch to watch tv. It was 10:00pm when I was hit with the "wait what" feeling again although this time when I sat up, I felt a pop which quickly followed by the ungodly Niagara Falls of amount of liquid rushing out of my body better known as my water breaking.

All I could do was say the words "my water just broke" as deadpan as any scared shitless woman could do and waddle my way to the nearest bathroom to stand on all the towels within arms reach. Now what?! At the time my ex did not have a valid license. He had had yet another DUI and could not drive me to the hospital. I called my sister who lived an hour and a half away and cried for her to come get me and take me to the hospital. For all the massive emotions that were flooding my body at that moment, none of them were anger that my husband couldn't drive me the 20 minute drive to the hospital.

I didn't see things for what they were until now.

It often requires a life altering moment for us to look back on our lives and see things for what they really were, not what we hoped for them to be in the moment. The rearview mirror is no place to spend time looking when you are planning on driving forward, but the road you've traveled up until this point, if reviewed carefully, can show you the roads you need to avoid on your future journey. I had looked past so many things in the roller coaster of my life. Past the history. Past the addiction. Past the lying. Past the cheating.

I was navigating an unwinnable race because it felt like that was what was required to hold my world together, and then, without asking me permission, my world blew into a million shattered pieces. My business, the one I'd sacrificed so much for, was bankrupt. My marriage was over. My house was gone. My bank account was at zero, okay less than zero. In the midst of it all, watching everything I identified as my life burn to the ground, I stood in the glowing embers and found peace. Rather than clutching to the wreckage trying to salvage anything that resembled a way out, I simply stopped and allowed the flames to ravage it all.

There is a familiarity in chaos. This time it's different. This time I chose to exist inside of it, without fear, without a need to save anything except what was left of myself and above all else my daughter. I know we will survive, that's one of the silver linings of having been through so much. When you've lived the roller coaster of a relationship with an addict you have a deep understanding that this will be yet another cliff you have scaled. You understand that just because you have been blessed with another day on this planet that isn't a guarantee it will be one without struggle. The road out of these woods is rarely traveled without tremendous roadblocks and detours; however; you still have the ability to drive.

There are many moments that I allow myself to feel the sting of loss. There's power in the tears that randomly spring up. Have you heard Tori Kelly's version of Hallelujah…come on now, no one can make it through that while driving alone in the dark at Christmas! More often I fend off the waves of negative thoughts and dodge the emotional landmines that are out there waiting for me and I focus all my thoughts, all of my energy, on the path forward. Sitting with a new peace, a different kind of peace that helped me to live simply in the day for the day instead of worrying about what the day would bring. The words I wanted to say to you as you navigate your own journey out of a toxic relationship crashed around in my head and flooded my heart. This book, its pages, are filled with the things I need for you to know.

Oftentimes while we are in the storm of someone else's addiction, someone else's destruction, we are so hyper focused on looking for signs of the next bomb that will go off that we lose sight of the good things happening in our lives. I want you to remember what is good in your life, the smallest, most insignificant, but massively important things. The smell of fresh cut grass. The first bite of your favorite dessert. Blankets right out of the dryer. Strangers waving you on in traffic.

Puppy breath. Your favorite band in high school randomly coming on the radio. Laughing until you can't breathe anymore. A handwritten letter. I want you to remember that you don't need chaos to appreciate what is good in your life. It is still good despite it all. What I want you to know most of all is, I understand. I want to sit across from you right now and tell you that you are strong enough, you are brave enough, you are enough…and you will survive this. It will feel impossible. It will hurt. It will be the hardest damn thing you ever do, but it is possible for you to come out of this a better version of yourself.

Here's the thing, in this moment, as you read these words, you have a choice to make. You must choose to either allow this thing to swallow you whole or you choose to stand back up. It is possible for you to move on. It is possible for you to not only survive, but to thrive despite, and more importantly because of, the terrible things you've endured.

I've watched so many people go through the hardest trials in life. A friend who lost his brother days before he should have been coming home from fighting in a war. Parents who lost their child to cancer. You can navigate your way out of this place in your life and be a better version of the scared driver who started the journey.

You get to choose how you come out of this. Will you allow it to steal the best parts of you? Will you become bitter? Will you live the rest of your life filled with worry about someone else's demons? Or will you fight for your own life?

Without a doubt, this, this moment, this part of your life is going to be a full out battle. You will have to fight for yourself, for your joy, for your peace, and for the love of the Lord, if you are a parent you must fight for your children. It is going to take everything within you to win this fight but it is possible. As you turn the pages of this book you will find them filled with every tool, tip, and guidance I can think of that helped me navigate my way through the most difficult time of my life. There isn't an emotion that has escaped me during this time and while writing about them and this journey isn't to gain anyone's sympathy or support, my hope is they are a connection for you to the truth. You can and will break free from the toxic cycle you are in. I write about my experience so that you may find your way out sooner than I did, and stronger than I ever was. The things I place here for you and the lessons I teach are all crafted from what helped me.

The real and often ugly experiences I trudged through are shared in hopes that it sparks the fire in your soul to stand up and move forward on your own path. Back to you. Better than before. I also share my story with you because for me, this act of writing it all here on these pages, means the decision I made many years ago, in my car, at a stoplight next to a grocery store, and all the decisions after weren't just leading me down a path of heartache and disappointment. They led me here to you. For all the tears, the silent screams, the embarrassment, the fear, I believe how I show up now and how I deal with all the hard parts of the life I've lived is the only real thing I get to solely choose for myself. And I choose better for myself. I choose better for my daughter.

What will you choose? I believe you are here reading this book today because inside of you, there is a spark of strength you didn't realize you had and I'm so damn proud to be here with you.

It's time to turn that spark into a whole raging fire, it's time to take action.

What Comes First

1
SEE YOURSELF

One of the most difficult parts of breaking free from a toxic relationship, especially one where there are factors of addiction, narcissism, and abuse (I hear you friends who just said "or all of the above" to themselves!) is the hard realization that many parts of who you are have changed. More often than not, when you come through any kind of trauma experience you come through with a totally different mindset and with different daily values. At the outset of the decision to walk away, we look at what is happening to us through the lens of who we are now, not who we were before. Most of our thoughts are ruled by the person we've become, not the person we once were.

It's like at the end of the Deathly Hallows when Harry Potter, no longer the meek and confused boy who lives in the cupboard under the stairs, decides he must go face Voldy alone instead of together with his trusty sidekicks and walks to what is surely going to be his death at the hand - er' wand - of his life-long nemesis. He does so filled with strength and courage because of experiences he faced fighting his way through life. He had become a different version of himself and so have you. You've moved through an experience of trauma, and chaos, and struggle but just like Harry, your sense of self, the you that makes up your core thoughts and feelings, well that self is still the you who you always were, we just have to find it.

Before you tackle the complete emotional upheaval that healing requires, you must come to terms with your true self. Not the projection of you, not the masked version, the real and most stripped down version of yourself. In order to find the person you once were you have to determine which costume you've been wearing.

In my experience, there are three different kinds of identity masks a person puts on when they are in a toxic relationship:

The first is: **The Do-er** - Always focused on creating the next task, the new project, the to-do list. The second is: **The Shadow** - Content to keep quiet, much more comfortable not being seen. And the third is: **The Positivity Pusher** - Never has a bad day, there's nothing to see here but rainbows and sunshine.

Let me explain this with a bit more personality.

Nearly thirteen years ago, sitting at the airport gate waiting after yet another delay, I was overcome with discomfort. Of course the hours my body had spent becoming one with the gate side rigid chair covered with a cushion as thin as my patience caused a physical discomfort that would require a visit to Dr. Derek, my chiropractor, but the real discomfort was deep in my mind. I had been on a work trip with my bosses and a few coworkers and just had spent the past few days doing my best to hold in my anger while pretending to be invested in a company and leaders that I had lost all respect for.

There's much more to that story but that is for another time in another book, the underlying connection here is that my boss had fired my husband just two months prior to this trip and he was back at home with our eight month old daughter spending his time "caring" for her while I was away. In reality he had been spending his time caring for her by playing video games and getting high. This was not the first time he had been fired in our marriage, more like the fourth. I was angry at everyone. Just before we finally were called to board our flight home, I had a lightning bolt moment that I had mastered at this point. An idea. The fix. We would start our own company and take control of our own lives. I quickly called my ex to tell him I was finally headed home and snuck in a "oh and we are going to start our own company as soon as I get home" before hanging up. It was that quick and we did just that. Was it an overnight solution? No, it took almost a year of insanity to be realized. But, without question, I knew that I forced this plan to come to life to ensure, or at least I thought so at the time, no boss could ever fire my ex again.

The first identity mask, The Do-er, is one I am intimately familiar with. This mask is my own and the one I've worn proudly for a decade. How often have you faced the question "What do I do now?" and swiftly moved as far away from the deeper answer that this question was truly asking you only to create any type of diversion you could come up with? A new job. New city, new hobbies, new church…a new baby. I can't begin to recall the amount of times I navigated one of the crisis moments in my relationship by creating something that would distract from the actual situation I faced. If you too wear the Doer mask, you have likely faced many similar moments. Friend, I need you to hear me right now, you no longer need to come up with the way through anyone's darkness but your own. You are not responsible for the solution to anyone else's problems. You are singularly responsible for you.

If the first and second identity masks were siblings, these would be the two that absolutely have nothing in common and don't get along at family gatherings. If the first creates all the solutions to one's problems, the second, **The Shadow,** wants nothing to do the problems at all. To describe this another way, let's take a look at it like this…

From the time I was a young girl I have always hidden from my parents. Not literally, except that one time I pretended to run away from home, and not who I am as a person, but I've hidden anything that could be perceived as wrong or more importantly when I knew I would be on the receiving end of words that made me feel as if I had disappointed them. (More on that juicy part of healing later.) On several occasions when things were rocky in my marriage; we had had a huge fight, he had started drinking more openly, things were rough at work, and primarily without my making a conscious decision to do so, I would all out ghost my parents. Every day, as a reflex reaction I make a call to my mom to check in. Oddly enough it almost always coincides with the exact time my sister has also called for her daily check-in. But, I digress. These calls are largely filled with nothingness. How was the day? Who's up to what in the family. What's for dinner? Okay. Okay. Uh huh. Okay. Bye. Every single day. Unless of course something's up. Then and only then these calls are put on indefinite pause. I simply don't call and for the first few days, neither does my mom. I can't tell you if that's her knowing to give me space or not, that's her story to tell, but this inevitable pause always signals something is afoot.

Here's the thing, I don't naturally ignore fires. I'm more apt to be the one to see the fire well before it is burning the building down and jumping to squelch the flames except in the singular case that I feel as if I will be looked at through discolored glasses. If what is swirling around me could possibly paint me in a light that causes reality to shine too bright, I am out. How many of us have hidden from the world entirely when things have gotten sideways? How many of us have chosen to find comfort in staying distant from everyone and everything because we are afraid, ashamed, embarrassed by our lives? If you find yourself wearing this identity mask, I see you back there in the shadows. I know how it feels to find guilt and blame on my own shoulders when the actions that caused the chaos are not my own. I can tell you right here and right now, nothing positive will come from you staying hidden away. You are far too beautiful of a soul to hide in the shadows of someone else's demons.

The third identity mask is one that is worn by many and is not uniquely tied to the topic we are speaking of. In an age of sharing every moment of your life online, if and only if you have the perfect angle of your avocado toast or the perfect selfie lighting coming from the golden hour sunlight in the carpool line…I'm talking to you Bold Glamour filter…it is far too often that we paint the image we want to be seen, not the one that truly is. **The Positive Pusher** identity mask requires an all out war on our negative thoughts, an assassination of our problems by simply refusing to acknowledge they are in fact there in the first place. This mask in particular can be outwardly perceived as, well, positive when in fact it can be the most damaging.

When the wheels started to fall off the bus I was driving with our business, I was terrified for all kinds of reasons. This wasn't an overnight disaster, to be honest it was a slow erosion over time, one that at some points was so slow it didn't seem like anything was in jeopardy at all and other times felt like I was holding my weak hands on the pin of a grenade. Our business specifically was tied to an image of exceptionalism. I say image because while our services were tangible, the perception of our company was what clients and colleagues bought into. They were sold uniquely on who we were, not necessarily what we did. The tiny fissures that would eventually make way for the larger craters to take hold showed up years before the final blow, and I saw each and every one of them. I was, and most painfully still am, the face of the company. While many knew my ex was my business partner as well as my husband, I was the face and name associated with all things good and all things bad…and there was a truck load of bad.

Our employees had a front row seat to our dysfunction and while they may have understood the problems within to be held by two parties, at the end it still came back to one. During each storm and even in the eye of each hurricane we went through, I placed my focus on creating an "everything is fine" culture. Image meant everything and it was suffocating everyone. My mantra would become that controlled chaos was normal. Chaos is simply chaos. Not once would I allow a word of negativity to exist, unless I was the one painting the matte black twist on the story. Did something happen at an event? Guess what, we are still better than our competitors. Did my ex drink and disappear today at work? Oh, he had something he needed to take care of offsite. Was the public bashing my ex on social media because of a fight over racism with an employee? No problem, I'll remove him from all online media and push content of the events we've done with minority groups and of our POC employees. You guys, it makes me sick to my stomach to even think about all the positive twists I crafted because of the dumpster fires he threw the match on. While I often put on this identity mask I was simultaneously wearing it with my Doer mask and became a completely blind and wildly ineffective leader.

I'm writing this for you now so you can highlight it, write it out yourself and look at it daily, memorize this, please please remember this: false positivity is always worse than honest negativity. If someone is causing heavy things to happen in your life, it is not your job to carry the weight. Trust me, the awareness of the real things, no matter what you do to try to paint a positive picture of them, will be self evident in your life. And while they may have very little to do with who you really are as a person, the pain caused in order to hold on to such things is not the reality of a healthy life.

Please know it is possible and frankly, likely, that you have taken on more than one of these identity masks and wear them interchangeably given the situation you are faced with. What masks are you carrying with you because you have had to be ready for the next bomb going off? How are the masks you are wearing changing your decision making? The reality is that each and every time you've chosen to place one of these masks on yourself you've altered your real identity. And while no one could come through something like you have without a shift in their being, it is vitally important to find the core of you because that, that place, that is where healing is found.

What I need for you to take with you from this chapter is that you are more than the masks you are wearing. Your real identity, the one who would never allow a friend to willingly cover up for their abuser, the one who knows not working on the actual injury never heals the full wound, and the one who like Harry, can see that despite of, in fact because of, the experiences you've faced you are stronger and more aligned with your true self than ever before. Take off your masks and see the work that needs to be done as the truest version of yourself.

Tips to remember:

Face The Mirror: Have the courage to face it all. The good, the bad, the unspeakable, you must pull yourself up by your bootstraps and find even the smallest amount of courage to face this journey of self head on. There is absolutely nothing good that will come staying stuck in the place you are in now. The only way out is through and so through we will go, together. Do not add a filter to what you see in your reflection. It is simply what it is. And remember, you must look in your review mirror in order to successfully navigate to your destination.

Let It Go: On occasion and only ever with as much conviction as you can muster, it is not only necessary but completely required to let all your emotion out, all at once, with a scream or a cry or a full on M'Lynn at Shelby's funeral fit if it is warranted. (That won't be the last reference to the holy grail that is Steel Magnolias, you're welcome.) The fact of the matter is that you have countless moments of emotional turmoil that have built up inside you and you deserve a release. A single moment to literally let it all go. So, go ahead, scream like Sally Fields, take a whack at Ouiser if you have to, then pull yourself together and move forward.

Seeing Yourself: The experiences you've endured have changed you; however; you are still you. Acknowledging which identity mask you've been using to cope with reality is crucial to breaking free and regaining your true self. When you are faced with yet another roadblock, keep the three main masks in mind: doers avoid conflict, shadows are consumed by conflict, and positive pushers deny conflict exists.

2
RECOGNIZING YOUR FEAR

It is important that we spend time talking about the feeling of fear because most of you who are reading this book are doing so stuck in a place of fear. You are in the beginning or maybe the middle of your journey through fear and are navigating the wide range of emotions that come along with it. I say this because it's vital to recognize that staying in a place where fear holds on to us is not a path of healing. We must, and I mean must, move through fear. It's entirely possible that you've been living with a feeling of fear for so long it feels as normal as brushing your teeth.

It feels more normal for you to exist within fear than it would be to know any other form of daily life. Fear of the next fight. Fear of him stumbling in from the garage again. Fear of not knowing where she is. Fear that you are not strong enough. Fear of losing everything.

When I was staring down the days of closing my business, I was consumed with fear. Each night I'd toss and turn knowing that if I went to sleep it was highly likely I'd have the good fortune to wake up in the morning and that meant I'd have to face the possibility that it was the day I had to say goodbye to it all. I had already made the decision to end my marriage at this point and knew there was no choice but to close the doors of our business, but that one final break had me riddled with fear. What helped me most was to understand the dangerous mindsets that come along with fear. I hope it will help you too.

I think of fear in these terms: **F**orgetting My Values; **E**liminating My Personal Power, **A**voiding Conflict, **R**ationalizing The Irrational. For me, these mindsets are what triggered me to stay within my fear. They are incredibly powerful and often times our true selves hide inside these things we can't or are scared to face.

In order to understand fear for what it truly is, I'd like to share with you how it shows up for me. Remember, I'm a planner by nature so breaking things down in detail to consume them is how I process best.

F - Forgetting My Values

In this sense, values by definition means your principles or standards of behavior and your specific judgment of what is important in your life. When was the last time you stopped and asked yourself "what matters to me?" I wish this one had been the first that I questioned when I began to realize my relationship had crossed over a line that it was never coming back from. I wish I had cared enough about myself to simply ponder what I truly valued in my life. Instead it took me coming face to face with a security team at my door while in the Grand Floridian Resort at Walt Disney World to start to digest what had happened to the standards I held for my life and for my daughter. In the midst of my daughter's 10th birthday trip to her favorite place in the world, my husband chose to hide in the hotel bar and drink bourbon until he passed out. Not a little passed out, passed out so much so that they believed he was in need of Narcan and when that didn't wake him they took him to the hospital.

Can you imagine the families coming through the lobby while this man in a Mickey Mouse t-shirt is being carried away on a stretcher because he's that drunk. It makes me want to throw up. While the security guard, the police officer, and two hotel managers politely asked me if I knew of any drug activity going on in our hotel room, my newly ten year old daughter sat on her bed wondering where her dad was. All I could muster was "not that I'm aware of" to every question as I stared straight at the officer's body cam wondering when I had gone from police offiers daughter to person on the investigation footage. When I went back in the room I tried to distract my daughter as best I could with room service and a movie but my mind was racing. Every thought was formed in a question. "When did I become the parent who was okay with exposing her child to this?" "Why am I okay with being lied to?" "What am I teaching my daughter to be okay with?" I wonder if you've asked yourself these questions too. In one of the worst moments the values I held long ago showed up like waves crashing against the shore. Continuously reminding me of the standards of life and behavior I had once held for myself I had simply forgotten to uphold.

Eroded over the course of my relationship and while not intentionally ignored, they were no longer part of my core being and I was ashamed of that. The values we once held are still just as meaningful. Your beliefs on what behaviors are acceptable and not are still just as important to your central being, you just need to acknowledge them as so. If this is something you are struggling with, ask yourself what is true for you. Are you okay with cheating? Are you okay with manipulation? Imagine the younger version of you, before you began your relationship, and ask yourself if you could see the whole of your life as it is now, is it a life you would want. The values you once held deserve to be remembered. You deserve to see them lived out in your life. Fear has navigated its way in between you and your values.

E - Eliminating My Personal Power

The next mindset that fear creates comes in the form of an attack on the very things that make you, you, and is especially true when we are in a relationship with a narcissist. This is what I found myself buried inside of when I realized I was hiding what I really wanted to project to the world because of someone else's behavior. I felt physically restrained by his actions and unable to claim the things that were really meant for me.

Each one of us is born with a unique gift that is ours and ours alone. Deep within us a skill or trait is embedded in the core of who we are, something that is special and meant only for us. Some are more outward and show up in big ways, imagine Michael Jordan or Peyton Manning. Other times, and more often than not, the gifts are subtle yet burn just as bright inside our souls. Think of it this way. I have a friend who came into my life in a way that is as twisted as both of our stories. She was hired in my company for a very part-time front of house role and because of one of my ex's spirals was later promoted to take over many of his responsibilities. You can imagine it was awkward at best for both of us. As years went by we experienced extreme changes and many mission impossible moments together. We were bonded. While her obvious skills were found keeping our office from drowning on a daily basis, what wasn't obvious was that she is deeply creative and imaginative. I realized this for the first time when we were planning our company's annual staff party. She lit up like a kid on Christmas morning when we started discussing what we should do for the event. Ideas were spinning around the table and as I was sitting across from her all I could do was think to myself, I had no idea she enjoyed planning and designing. Not a clue. She had hidden it well.

And so I let her run with it. There were instances over the following years that her passion for creativity bubbled to the surface. It occasionally would come up in conversation as she witnessed the chaos swirling in my own life and felt comfortable to share her own. We have many similarities and while her story is her own to tell, I think it's important in this moment to share that what I saw in her life also echoed in my own and I believe it could be true for you. She was diminishing her true passion, her true gift, because of the actions of others. Fear crept into her life and stole away her personal power. The thing that makes her shine the brightest was a very dim light now and even while sitting day in and day out in the heart of a company built specifically to house creative souls, she kept herself small and shied away from allowing others to see her unique gift.

Fear had taken over control of her innermost thoughts and destroyed any positive self image she may have had about her personal power. You may not be a world class athlete. You may not be an actress or a high profile politician. Your gift, the thing that makes you feel joy in the depths of your soul, that thing that comes so natural to you, deserves to be seen, be heard, be shared. You are worthy of it and the world is better for having you use it to the fullest.

Hiding it because of someone else's opinion of you or because their actions are louder than yours, won't serve you. What it will do is rob you of your joy and rob the rest of the world around you of experiencing the best version of you. Fear has come to take your personal power away and you must, with all you have, fight for it to be yours.

A -Avoiding Conflict

Avoiding Conflict. Ew. Just uttering the words makes me scrunch up my nose in awkwardness like that time in the first grade when I got caught after having just cut off all my 1980's bangs with my brand new pair of scissors and quickly made the decision that it was a great idea to try to use my foot to scoot the freshly cut blonde locks under Carrie's desk while proclaiming there was no way I had just clipped them myself. Sorry about that Carrie. Here's the thing, no one really likes conflict. As a general rule, I have spent most of my life trying to stay as far away from conflict as I can. I don't like when others are upset and more specifically when I know they are upset with me because of something I've done. But this fear mindset goes far beyond simply not being comfortable when others are unhappy, it cuts much deeper.

In this case, not only are we choosing to shy away when we know someone is upset, we are making the choice to condone their actions even when they are harmful to our own wellbeing. I'm sorry to be the one to say this to you, but I care about you enough to make sure you hear the truth - you not standing up against your partner's darkness is self abuse. When you ignore the latest relapse or say nothing when they've lost another job, fear is keeping you stuck in this cycle. And friend, until you decide today is the day you are putting on your battle armor to defend yourself you will always be in the cycle. Fear of their retaliation. Fear of what others will think. Fear of being alone. No matter the reason, and there are thousands of them, fear will push you to avoid conflict. Trust me when I say these words: you are worth standing up for. You are worth calling out their actions. You are worth the fight. You ARE worth it!

R - Rationalizing the Irrational

In the journey through and out of a toxic relationship we become expert
storytellers. Some are more like epic novels filled with teeth clenching details page after page of horror'd retellings of events while others are straight forward autobiography-esk tales of sorrow.

Most often the stories we tell are to ourselves and no matter which of us is the author, each shares a common denominator at some point along the way. These stories rarely contain the entire truth. I don't mean this to say you, or I, are a liar. I'm not saying what's happened to us isn't real. What I know for sure is that it is just as likely you will find a diamond buried in your backyard as it is that you recount each detail of your relationship exactly as it was. More likely, you've cushioned your partner's misdeeds. No matter how much we've been told there is not a one size fits all standard for abuse we rarely look straight at our own circumstances and measure them with proper importance. How many times have you said the words to yourself or out loud to a listening ear: "others have it so much worse" or "it's not like he hits me or anything like that."

The terrible truth of the matter is most people who have been on the receiving end of the consequence of someone else's toxic behavior for a long period of time experience a shift in their own thinking that promotes playing down their pain or suffering so that the day to day is more bearable. For example: your partner drinks alcohol every day but they don't drive once they've started drinking so you rationalize that their functioning alcoholism isn't as bad as if they were drinking and driving, or your partner has a highly stressful job and to cope the stress and anxiety they smoke marijuana every day when they get home from work "just to chill out" but they aren't doing hard drugs so you've rationalized that their drug use isn't that bad. Friend, here me now, if you have used or are currently using the phrases "isn't as bad" or "isn't that bad"... .it's bad. And bad just is.

No amount of rationalizing will make bad things good. All of the justifications, all of the excuses, all they are doing is keeping you stuck in your fear. Keeping you stuck in the cycle and in the pain. Not once will the altered stories of your reality prove to serve you. Your story, with all the real bumps and valleys and cliffhangers, with all the horrific details and sorrow filled moments, deserves to be told and that begins with you facing each and every part with truth. You can no longer sit in fear, no longer rationalize the irrational pieces of your puzzle. Your path forward is through and that includes narrating the details of your story exactly as they are.

Tips to remember:

Apply pressure to the wound: You've watched enough medical drama television episodes to know the first thing you do when you come across someone with a trauma wound is…apply pressure. (And then pick right back up with helping your best friend's sister's dog sitters love triangle, but I digress.) I'm certain its listed at the top of things to do on the "How to save a life on tv" checklist and the same thing is true when you are working through your own trauma. When you recognize you have a gaping life threatening wound in your relationship, apply pressure to the areas you know are the hardest for you to overcome. For me, that looked like recognizing my fear for what it really was and doubling down on my own healing by putting my entire energy towards the underlying mindsets I was choosing for myself. By putting pressure on those areas, I was giving myself a path forward.

Find your few: As much as the work to be done here is yours and yours alone, it is infinitely important that you have someone to share and process with. Finding the few people who support you without judgement and without their own motives is a necessary part of healing. I learned a hard lesson as I walked through the days of leaving my husband and shutting down our business. Most of those I wanted to turn to for support and for validation were truly there to hear the latest gossip or to ask questions that served their own life. Did they love and support me? Yes. Was it from a place that was held in place by their own intentions? Also yes. I realized I had to pull back to the small circle that I knew was there simply for me. My few. If you don't have people in your life where you can find the freedom to simply be just as you are and how you need in the moment, I would encourage you to find a support group online where anonymity might just be of help. One thing I know for sure, the roller coaster of emotions that come along with working through this kind of journey cannot be locked up. The more you work to keep them in, the more they work to boil over on you in the worst possible moment. Find your few that will help you keep things cooking in the pot, not splattering all over the kitchen.

Make up your mind: Right now as you read this book you possess the single most important thing needed to make it through the excruciating journey you're on. Your mind. Your thoughts. Your own internal dialog will make or break you in this and in any other difficult thing you will face in your lifetime. The things we tell ourselves, whether truthful or not, determine our outcome. I'm not suggesting that a positive mindset is all we will need here, but I am telling you without it, you will fail. Fighting every day, and sometimes every moment of the day to choose to take back control of your mindset is the only requirement of success. It's important to note, your mindset will need a new set of things to support new patterns of thinking. Change doesn't come without a cost.

3

THE THING ABOUT RESPONSIBILITY

This entire book is written within the keen perspective of someone who has been through the process of breaking free from an addict's abusive behavior because, well, that is the exact experience I've lived in. As I've crushed away at the keyboard I've realized that there is a completely separate perspective to recognize as it is one that often holds power over us. Their perspective.

The likelihood of you having come through your relationship without shouldering some of the responsibility of wrong-doing is just as high as it is that you are an alien from another planet brought to Earth to read and analyze this literary work of wonder.

Perhaps you were the one to instigate arguments. Maybe you yelled in front of your kids. Or you were the one who slapped your partner when they were screaming in your face again. Did you cheat? Maybe you lied? I can't begin to know what exactly happened in your life or how specifically you contributed to the turmoil in your relationship but what I do know is this - if you feel guilt, embarrassment, or shame about it now, it's time to recognize it for what it is and let it go. You are not required to receive forgiveness from your partner for the things you did to cause strife in your relationship but you are required to forgive yourself.

You holding on to any number of negative feelings surrounding your own actions will not change where you are today. There is no amount of self-loathing that will rework the past. All we can do in the here and now is recognize it for what it was and understand why we did the things we did so that we might never do them again. I know as you are reading this right now you are surfing your memories of every word or action you used to cause your partner pain. I know as you read these words only some of them are sticking because you are caught up in reliving that moment when you lashed out, when you lost yourself. I am begging you, come back to me and hold on to these words right here…hear them deep in your soul… you must forgive yourself and let it go.

Your wrong-doings don't make theirs right. Their perspective of your troubles doesn't make it your truth.

Two and a half years before my marriage ended the abuse I had always downplayed as normal arguments of a married couple shifted and became physical. It was about 10 o'clock, I had finally gotten our daughter to sleep and headed downstairs to find my ex. It had been a weird night with him. At this stage in my daughter's life she needed a parent to sit with her as she fell asleep, for almost an hour, sometimes more, every single night, and so I had been upstairs with her for quite awhile. What I look back on now and see is that her troubles falling asleep were tied to a previous situation involving her as a peacefully sleeping three year old, myself, and her intoxicated father, but we'll get into that story later. When I got downstairs I didn't find my ex in the living room which is where he would have been normally, I found him in the garage, which was never a good sign. I knew within a millisecond of opening the door leading from our laundry room into the garage that he was drunk and I took the first step towards him with searing hot angry words coming out of my mouth. He met me halfway across the garage with the sarcastic and sneering tone he falls into when he's been drinking slurring through the air.

There were merely inches between us as we screamed pointlessly at each other. And then, I raised my hands. I did so to block him from coming closer into my personal space because somewhere behind my anger I felt threatened, but, you better believe I was ready to smack his bourbon soaked mouth away from me. Before I even got my hands up, he had my arms tight in his grip, twisting them towards my body, and then shoved me backwards. I tripped over a pile of tools that he had left on the floor and badly injured my foot and my leg. I can't tell you what happened next or what words were said immediately after. Everything in my memory stops there. What I did know in that moment was there was no amount of justifying I could do with this new fact about my relationship that would make it seem normal so I knew I would make the choice to say nothing to anyone about what had happened. To the outside world, I would ignore it, but inward, that was a different story entirely. The fact of the matter was my internal thoughts replayed the encounter in my head every minute of the day for weeks and I did so not because I was recounting his actions, I did so because I was searching for reasons to blame myself. Never when I relived this moment was I focused on his actions, I was always focused on my own.

When I did bring it up to him, he blamed me and I not only allowed it, I believed it. That became the hamster wheel that had been placed in my head always revolving around my own actions in this situation… "What if I hadn't gone out there in the first place. I shouldn't have yelled. I shouldn't have raised my hands. Was I going to smack him?" It took me years to recognize his manipulation and more importantly that I needed to forgive myself.

I'm using this moment in my past to help you if you find yourself in a similar situation. If you should find yourself living in a world of blame and guilt over your own actions, believing you are responsible for the things that have happened to you, it's time to stop. If you've sincerely looked at the whole of your circumstances and truly worked to change, it's time to forgive yourself too. It isn't your responsibility to carry the weight for the rest of your life. It is your responsibility to see yourself forward.

Another way this might show up inside your journey is the responsibility other people might believe you are required to carry. The people who look down on you because you chose divorce.

The people who tell you if you really loved someone you would stick by them when they are struggling most. The people that reach out because they are concerned about what your church will think, or your neighbors will say, or your family members might believe. The people that when your partner's troubles are mentioned, say "well, she allowed it" or "he's just as much to blame." The perspective of the people around you can be a blessing but sometimes, sometimes it can be a curse. It's important to know humans, for better or for worse, have opinions and those opinions are just that, their opinions. They don't now or ever in the future change the things you've experienced in your life.

It's YOUR life.
Here is my response to those who may have opinions about what is your responsibility: I will not allow your opinions, judgements, or expectations impact the way I protect my values and live my own life. When I made the choice to walk away from my marriage and my business, I made the choice to hurt a lot of people. I made the choice to hurt my husband. I made the choice to hurt my daughter. I made the choice to hurt my employees, my clients, my professional relationships. I hurt so many people and I knew I had responsibility in the demise of both.

While it hurt like hell, and even with the months of hearing the opinions of others blasted all over the internet and the nightly news…yes it made the news…we are still digging deeper ya'll….I was willing to be the villain of the story because I knew I was the hero of mine and more importantly my daughters. I knew the decision I made was the only possible way for us to come through the darkness we were living in and be healthier and happier. The reality about your responsibility is this: you cannot hold yourself in a place of pain because of the opinions others have about what you have done or should do in the future and you must walk alway from anyone who makes you feel otherwise.

Tips to remember:

Lessons from Pre-K: Do you remember the first time you were told two wrongs don't make a right? Me either but I'm going to generalize here and say it was likely a lesson about doing the right thing that we were taught as early as our preschool years. This was also about the time that we were learning that we were responsible for our own actions and that blaming others wasn't a characteristic of an upstanding human. Isn't it interesting how many of us have forgotten the fundamental truths we were taught in our earliest years. It's time to recall the teachings of Mrs. Perkins and parents everywhere. You are wholly responsible for your own actions and yours alone, not your partners, not your family members, not your friends, not your coworkers, no one but yourself and you cannot make someone else's wrongdoings right by making bad decisions yourself.

You don't need their forgiveness to be forgiven: Oooh my, this one…well…it's complicated. At the heart of most human-beings is a deep desire, a need, to be forgiven. It's the very root of most of our religious beliefs and one that trips up even the most righteous among us. So, breaking this one down is going to be difficult. I want you to keep in mind a few things when it comes to forgiveness. One, forgiveness is not always a two way street. You are not guaranteed forgiveness from someone else even if you have given it to them. This can be one of the biggest roadblocks you will face on your path out of a toxic relationship. You have to choose to be okay with not being forgiven. Two, your forgiveness of someone who's wronged you is just as much about you as it is about them. Choosing to forgive allows your soul to move on, not necessarily theirs. You deserve forgiveness but most of all you deserve to forgive.

4
FANTASY VS. REALITY

When my daughter was seven years old she proclaimed her undying love for none other than Peter Pan. And not just any Peter Pan, THE Peter Pan, the one she had met on more than one occasion on trips to Walt Disney World. This Pan was the only Pan. She had played tag with him outside Cinderella's castle, stood in 150 degree temperatures to take a photograph with him…okay just kidding but Florida mid-day in the summer feels like the surface of the sun…and she required that we hunt him down on any occasion we could. Not only did she proclaim that this boy who never grows up was hers and hers alone, she did so with a conviction stronger than my undying love for wasting money at Starbucks.

This girl doubled down. She prepared a wedding ring for Mr. Pan and refused any conversation that would imply he was in fact not her boyfriend. So, what's a reasonable mother to do? I played along, but not just casually, I fully embraced this fantasy for her. I wrote notes on her bathroom mirror from Peter and started a daily journal so she and Peter could talk back and forth about their overnight adventures in Neverland while she was fast asleep. She lived for those notes, truth be told I lived for those notes, but as the months passed by she slowly let it show that she knew it was me keeping this folly alive and while she was in no way admitting it or ready to let it all go, she would poke through the thin line between fantasy and reality and tell me the unspeakable without having to tell me anything at all.

Have you ever stopped to think about all the things you've once believed with full conviction that now you know are untrue? As children there are many but what about as you've grown and in your adult life? Chances are there are many things that at one point in your life you've believed, things that now that you know better, seem completely ridiculous. But here's the thing, at the time you believed them, they weren't ridiculous at all they were your truth and while the thing you believed to be true may not have been made up of facts, it was true through your perspective.

It was the way you saw things in your life and even though it could have been something as far fetched as marrying the Peter Pan you know from running around Disney World, your reality was shaped by your perspective. I think it's important that we spend some time working through the murky water of how your perspective impacts how you come through the journey you are on today. Your perspective, on any topic really, isn't necessarily rooted in truth, but more likely is formed because of things you've experienced in your past and how they've impacted what you think about them. The thing to keep in mind here is that you are in control of your perspective. You get to choose it, good or bad. The you that you've chosen to be today, is in control of the beliefs you hold about whatever you've gone through in the past, and while understanding this won't change the things that have happened, it can help you to adjust how you see them leading to a more healthy and happier life regardless of what's going on around you.

There are a few key parts to understanding how your perspective can help or hinder how you move through healing. It's also important to note that you and you alone have to do this work, no one else can do it for you. That's the thing about perspective, it's yours.

The more common way to think about perspective is how it relates to your attitude or point of view towards something. Each of us has a particular attitude or point of view about literally everything. Does the topic of money interest you or make you recoil from the conversation? Do you love margarita night with your girlfriends or does an invitation to drink make you nervous? Are you the first to watch the latest Hallmark movie or do shows that focus on relationships make you uncomfortable?

The way we feel about these questions, the way we see these situations, and many like them is based on the collective experiences we've had in the past. While we aren't making conscious choices about how we feel, our subconscious views them and makes a judgement about whether it is good or bad. Going a step further, our entire body picks up on what our brain just told us was true and now we are fully invested in how to react. Are margaritas bad for us? No. Is the completely predictable rom-com harmful? No. How about money, is money wrong? Also no. know you know these things. I know you realize what is real and what is skewed. Sadly, our experiences in the past have caused us to have reactions we aren't even consciously choosing.

Those intense feelings of fear and uneasiness are conditioned responses that will continue for the rest of our lives if we don't choose to create a different perspective. Right now, everything that is happening in your life, all the chaos and uncertainty and trauma, it is all viewed through a lens of either positive or negative perspective. The things that are happening are very real, I'm not discounting them nor am I saying you should either. What I am saying is you possess an immense amount of power when you understand that you are subconsciously creating your reality through the experiences you've had in the past. Just as you choose which shirt to put on today, you can choose to see something as entirely negative or see it with positive pieces.

If your past experiences have conditioned you to see the negative in everything around you, it's time to shift your perspective. The pain you are living with today can be repositioned to the hope you feel for tomorrow. Some of us are in the midst of deep trauma. It's hard, no, it's damn near impossible to find a positive in the situation of someone being abused. Physical harm makes that even harder. But, there is positive in you here right now with me, reading these words, knowing the place you are in today isn't for you. Your perspective here, in this moment, can give you hope.

Your ability to see even the smallest positive, to shift where your perspective is in the moment and focus it in a new direction is powerful. One of the ways to begin adjusting your perspective is by taking a look at the scariest parts of our lives and viewing them for what they really are, not what we've altered them to be. Let's circle back to Cinderella's castle for a minute, I know, just stay with me here. Did you know that Disney's famed parks and most of their most iconic attractions are not exactly what they seem to be? Cinderella's castle, and more impressively Beast's castle are nowhere near as large as they appear to be. Even as you stand there taking countless photos of your children who have yet to actually smile for you, the famous landmarks in your foreground are nowhere near the size they seem. You see, part of the magic is actually in the design concept of forced perspective. Objects appearing bigger than they actually are when viewed from a specific place or point. They seem that big, and therefore they are, right?

What areas of your life are you viewing as bigger than they actually are? When I lay awake at night wondering what was going to happen when I knew the business wasn't going to survive and my marriage was officially over, I had to break down the scariest part of what was to come and view them from an entirely new perspective. They were huge, unscalable mountains when I first looked at them and then, somehow my view began to change. The things I saw happening to me, my home would be gone, my belongings gone, my reputation gone…when I changed the way I viewed these things and saw them not as unscalable mountains but as difficult climbs on the way to a much more peaceful summit, they simply ceased to matter as much anymore. I saw them not as things wholly negative and against me, but had to focus on how they could bring good to me, even if it was only a sliver of good. I had to see that from where I was standing the things I was facing seemed so much bigger than they actually were.

How can you change the way you view the current circumstances in your life? How can you stop the negative experiences in your past from keeping you stuck in pain and trauma? I believe if you break them down one by one you will find reality is much different than the fantasy we've designed.

Tips to remember:

Speaking of the Truth: More often than not we struggle to find truth on our own. We might see it, we may even acknowledge it, but to really find it and live in it, that's something else entirely. When my daughter was deeply living in the world of fantasy I saw her struggling to hold onto it with everything she had. Even with the cracks in the surface, like moments when she began to ask questions about Santa and the time she asked why she could see where a zipper was on a certain furry friend's back while we were at dinner at Chef Mickey's, she would quickly navigate away from the topic. She knew, but she had no desire to know. For a time, that was okay and I not only let her live there I fostered it. I would tell her things like "it's real to you so therefore it's real" or simply ask "what do you believe" and leave it at that. But, as she grew and I saw how this specific perspective could come to harm her, I knew it was my job to help her see things from a different angle, one that held all the truth but allowed her to choose what she did with that truth from there. It was just before Christmas when I pulled the bandaid off completely. You know, it's better to rip it off all at once than do it slowly, right?

Well, I had hoped so, and so I told her. Flat out told her. Santa's not real. Tooth fairy. Not real. Mickey Mouse. Not real. Peter Pan…..deep breath…not real. She was pissed. I expected tears and sadness but nope, she was angry and then she ignored it. We didn't revisit the topic until she brought it up weeks later when I was able to help her see that while all the things she believed were real lived inside her perspective, some of them weren't going to serve her to continue to believe were reality. In this case she knows it's okay to enjoy the fantasy but she can't get lost within it. In your case, I think it's important to know you might also need someone to help you see things that you believe to be true but that aren't serving your mission for a healthier happier life. You may see them, you may even know things aren't necessarily what you believe them to be, but it often takes someone on the outside to rip the bandaid off and help you see what's fantasy and not reality.

Support what supports you: This one is crucial but not groundbreaking new information. In order for us to maintain a changed perspective we must surround ourselves with influences that support the way we want to think and act. You've heard that or something like it before, but, I know it is always good to be reminded of it in our hardest seasons.

Choosing to give your energy and focus to the people and activities that show up with the attitude you want to have will impact your path. If you are going through something hard or are experiencing something difficult in your life and you surround yourself with affirmations of your hardship then you will only see the hard things. You lose out on the opportunity to view things in a different way and more importantly you lose out on the chance for better. Fill your days with things and people that show up for you in a positive way, not because the hard things don't deserved to be seen or acknowledged, but because you deserve the chance for happiness. You deserve the positive influence of others to lift you out of the darkness.

Someone has gone before you: It's important to keep in mind that someone somewhere in this world has gone through an experience similar to yours right now. I promise you, as unique as your situation feels to you, there is someone who has walked the road before you. Yes, there may be variations of the journey and for sure there are different experiences with them, but I can assure you that you are not alone. The good thing about someone else having experienced the pain that you feel now is that they have left clues and knowledge along the way for you to learn how best to navigate it yourself. Will each be helpful for you? Not likely. But, some will and some will be the exact thing you need to help you take the next step forward and then the next. If you can choose the mindset of accepting the lessons that are there to help you heal and you are willing to put yourself out there to be seen, you will find the help you need. Deciding you want to seek a different way of viewing things is the very first step of changing your vision for your future. Every step after that takes listening and learning but make no mistake, you can and you will if you choose to.

5

WHAT'S THE WORST THING THAT CAN HAPPEN?

Time for a confession. I am a worrier.

Car accident on the news? It's definitely one of my family members. Know someone taking a flight? I'm watching the flight online for any signs of trouble. Someone is sick? For sure researching the doctor caring for them and sending a Linkedin request to said doc juuuust in case.

I am a worrier, but let me clarify. I am not at all worried when it comes to taking big risks or living outside the bounds of normal. I encourage and have built my personal brand on the foundation of living in the awkward and standing inside risk, but, when it comes to worrying about day to day things. I'm a hot mess.

I worry about many things, the majority of them are not even real and I tell you this because it's important for us to talk about worry and fear. Yes, we've talked about fear before but in this sense I want to focus on the type of fear that sends you spiraling. The kind that causes your thoughts to jump from thinking one thought and then all of the sudden your heart is pounding and you are having hot flashes because your mind raced off to circle the drain of what ifs. This worry. This fear. It can be crippling. Most often it is a result of our brains being triggered to recall things we've experienced before that have caused us pain or hardship.

When a past experience is causing pain in the present we must first recognize we are no longer in control, our worry and our fear are, and then understand in order to move forward we must find the courage to take it back. For you to see progress past your fear, you must decide that there is something much greater at risk than the things you fear.

Take that in a minute. You must decide that there is something greater at risk than the things you fear most. You. You are far greater than anything you could possibly be fearful of. It's important for you to hear that correctly.

I'm not saying over time you will come to the realization that you were worth more than…no…I'm saying today, right this second, you must decide with full conviction and no doubt in your mind that you are worth so much more than anything you fear and to do so you will need to choose courage, every day.

Have you ever watched the movie The Sandlot? When my nephews were young I spent endless hours cuddled up with them watching this masterpiece. Over and over again we watched and learned how to make a proper S'more from the great Hamilton "Ham" Porter, laughing at Squint's shenanigans kissing Wendy Peffercorn, and understanding how courage can overcome even the scariest of beasts.

To me choosing courage in a season like you are going now through looks a whole lot like Benny the Jet Rodrigez choosing there was something greater at risk than any beast on the other side of the fence. He knew his friend needed him to show up with more courage than their collective fear and so he ran like only he could, jumped that fence, and schooled Hercules, better known as the Beast. In this scenario Benny knew this was about more than a baseball signed by the Great Bambino himself, it was about saving his friend's neck.

In your case, it's about so much more but the truth about courage and finding it for something bigger than our fear is still very much the same.

If you are struggling to find courage, and let's get real honest, we all are, it isn't because you don't have the ability to do so, it simply means you haven't established what is greater than your fear. In this time in your life, fear stands tall, it's a giant in your daily life. Fear of any number of things keeps you stuck in your pain, frozen in place not able to break free. It keeps you inside the cycle with your partner. It keeps you from leaving. It provides an unsafe comfort. It takes courage to find peace in being uncomfortable after your life has been rocked to its core.

To find the level of courage it takes to walk a path as big as the one you are on, you will need to let go of anything that provides comfort for you within the place that is causing you pain. Many of us believe the comfort of what we know - even though it is harmful to us - is better than the fear of what would happen to us, or our partners, if we left. While it's widely known but rarely spoken, it's true, and I too believed it for nearly twenty years. I had to strip away every comfort my relationship, my profession, my life provided to find the courage to not only believe my life was worth more but to do anything possible to protect it.

Friend, you will never find the courage to push past your fears if you don't make it an absolute necessity to do so. This change, it's hard. It's so hard, and in order for courage to find its way into your life, you are going to have to be willing to take on the thing that scares you most. I know it seems impossible. I know it ceases you with a gripping fear that leaves you timid and breathless. I also know this decision is one of the hardest anyone ever has to make and without something that is more important to you, you will stay exactly where you are. Only with courage as your center will you see all the things your life could be, should be.

Spending your life worrying and being fearful of what someone else may do next is no way to live. Spending your life afraid that things will never get better is almost always guaranteed that they won't. You must find what is greater and bond your courage to it as if your life depended on it, because it does.

Tips to remember:

Inches lead to feet: No one is asking you to run this marathon in record breaking time. Our situations are unique to us which means there are multiple variables that will change the course each of us takes and how long it takes us to complete it. There will be times for quick action and times when you need to slow down. It isn't the speed in which we take this journey that matters, it is only that we take it. Focus on one moment at a time, then one day, then a week, and a month. The time will string your actions together and you will find your inches of progress lead to feet of success in your journey.

Define your fear: I'm going to recommend something that has worked for me countless times in different seasons of my life when I've faced big decisions or moments where I needed motivation and momentum to serve my goal. When it came time for me to get honest with myself about what was holding me back, the things I feared most if I made the choice to leave, I used this trusted tool and found it immensely helpful. I keep a notebook with me at all times. In fact, I have several. One for big audacious dreaming ideas, one for tasks I need to get done, one for randomness…I love notebooks. In this case I found it helpful to literally write out the words of what I was worrying about most. I took out a special notebook I had been given, matte black with a black pen, and oh my is it gorgeous. It was perfect. I wrote out in very straightforward sentences what I was terrified of. "I'm afraid of leaving him and him getting worse." "I'm worried about what this will do to my daughter." "I'm don't want to be alone." "I am scared to death to lose my professional reputation." On and on. I wrote down everything I could think of and kept at it for days when things would pop up at random, you know how things just hit you out of nowhere. This brutally honest look at my life and what I would face if I truly made the decision to walk away was oddly cathartic and provided a road map for me through my fear. Once I had written down all the worst things I could think of it gave way for me to address my future actions as they related to each one. "I will lose all my possessions." became "Someday I will be able to have new things." The unknown may still have been unknown but in this case I had taken control of the what if's and built a plan for each of them.

6
GET OUT

I am going to level up this conversation a bit and before I do I want to give you fair warning. It's time that I get straight with you and in a way that goes further than motivation and moves right on to blunt, brutal, because someone has to do it, truth. Think of this part as going from a gentle nudge in the right direction to being prodded with a taser…except without the physical pain part. I know many say it can be counterproductive to be harsh with someone going through the trauma of a toxic relationship, and I get it, I do, but here's the thing, the people closest to you aren't going to tell you what needs to really be said. And so I will, even if it means it pisses you off. I'll stand in that gap for you.

Let's do this.

Friend, it's time to stop making excuses… and leave.

Listen, if you've picked up this book there's almost a 100% chance you are searching for validation and a way out. If you were looking for someone to help you fix things, or tips to save your relationship, you would have chosen a different resource. (If that was what you came here for, I'm immensely sorry, you've come to the wrong place.) I know you want to live a healthier, happier life. I know you want to stop all the chaos and heartache. I know this like the back of my hand because I've lived it…for an entire 13 year marriage. Through 4 DUIs, time in jail, faked counseling attempts, emotional abuse, physical abuse, having a child together, and ruining a business…I've lived it.

You must take the step to leave. I don't mean to start planning to possibly leave someday in the future. I mean, take the first step right now to be done, forever. This is me telling you right now what I wish I had listened to many years ago. You must find the courage to leave it all behind. If you are a parent this is especially true. You have the utmost responsibility to your children to leave immediately. No excuses.

And before you jump to thinking everyone's situation is different or not all of us are as privileged to be able to walk away, I get it, I do. I left with literally zero income, a negative bank account, no savings, and an overnight bag of clothes for my daughter and myself. Yes, I had the support of my family to ensure we were not homeless and I am forever grateful for that. I do realize others aren't as fortunate; however; there are resources available right now to help anyone who needs a way out. I want to be extremely clear, I am in no way suggesting that you should endanger yourself or ever put your children in jeopardy. I am; however; saying you can make this decision and that there is always a way to take safe, smart action if you truly want a better life. Even more so, I'm saying that your non-action on this matter is a self admission that you condone the type of life you and your children are living.

The evening prior to our wedding day we held a ceremony rehearsal, like most people do. I remember riding to the church with my parents and feeling like I was going to be sick the entire drive there. Just before we arrived we made a quick stop at the gas station to grab something to drink. As we pulled in I saw my ex's dad and step-mother were also in the parking lot. Seems like a cute coincidence, right?

It was just straight up awkward. Our families had never met and while the thoughts had been creeping up in my mind knowing how strange this would all be once the day finally came, I was skilled at playing whack-a-mole with any shred of a thought that could show the cracks in the foundation of our relationship. We got out of the car and exchanged the weirdest two minutes of pleasantries that have ever existed between humans. I can only imagine what my parents were thinking. The next two hours were filled with similar moments. To be honest, I don't think anyone there was comfortable with what was going on. As we were waiting on my two best friends to arrive in order to get things started, I filled the strange silences with as much staged laughter and levity that I could muster. Inside I was livid that they were late. At the time I felt hurt that they were blowing off something so important to me. I actually still don't know why they were running late but at the time it felt like I was being punished for doing something wrong. It was no secret that they didn't support our getting married let alone me even being in a relationship with him to begin with. They had witnessed all the ugly moments leading up to this day and try as they might to be there for me, I knew if they had a choice in my husband, he sure wasn't it.

As I look back now I know the anger I was feeling in the moment wasn't anger at all, it was shame. It's taken years of getting real with myself to fully admit what I knew standing there in that random church. I knew it was wrong. I knew it wouldn't last. I knew we would never recover from his addiction troubles and infidelity. What I didn't know was how long I would let him ruin me.

I'm not telling you all of this to gain your sympathies, I'm telling you because someone reading this book right now knows exactly how I felt that day. As sure as I am that my fingers are pounding away at this keyboard, I have no doubt that there is someone so wrapped up in avoiding the true thoughts they have about their life that they are willing to overlook the people they love who are also in pain because of it. Don't for a second think that your staying in the chaos of your relationship doesn't impact the people that love you. Don't be that selfish! Your family, your friends, especially your kids…they did not ask for this. You owe it to them to be better. You owe it to yourself to BE BETTER! I know it's hard and I know how afraid you are, but it will not get better unless you fight to make it that way. One right thing and then another.

That's all I'm asking you to do. It's time to get up and get moving. One minute at a time, do it for the people you love most, do it for yourself, because you have no other choice.

It's time to make the decision to leave. Full stop.

Tips to remember:

Disney always has the answers: I have an undying obsession with Disney. The movies, the music, the parks, but if we are being real honest my nerdy business brain is in love with the company operations as a whole. During one of the particularly hard days following leaving my entire life behind I found myself blubbering like a complete maniac after dropping my daughter off at school one morning. I'm talking can't catch your breath, snot running down my face, and stinging eyes crying so hard that I had to pull off on the side of the road to get myself together. What caused this random dramatic emotional explosion? Well, that thank you goes to Kristen Bell singing The Next Right Thing on the Frozen II soundtrack. You see, for months my daughter and I listened to Disney music every day on the 30 minute drive to her school.

We sang at the top of our lungs, shimmy and shake, and fully become one with the characters behind these tunes. At the time we were deep in Frozen II musical territory, this was just before Encanto came on the scene and well if you know, you know… we don't talk about Bruno… and Elsa and Anna, they were our carpool besties every morning. As the song got moving all I heard was this Disney princess turned Queen telling me that I had no choice but to do the next right thing and then the next if I was going to survive this. No, the concept and even some of the words are not new or original, but to me they became an anthem on the days I didn't have a clue what I was supposed to be doing. You see, when you break it down, it really is that simple. All you are responsible for are your own actions. On the darkest days, focus on only doing the next right thing and you will find the path into the light can be found. Oh, and thanks Anna.

Find Peace: There's no sense in hiding the fact that once you leave a toxic relationship, things will be intense for some time afterwards. I don't say that to scare you or dissuade you from making this decision, I say it because I will always bring blunt honesty to this conversation and I think it's important that you are prepared.

In the weeks after you leave your relationship it is vital that you create ways to find moments of peace. This will look different for every one of us but here are some things that helped me: find a podcast to listen to, create a peace playlist, read a book, binge watch a new show, rewatch a movie you love even if it's the 700th time you've watched it, retreat to a scalding hot bathtub and don't come out until the water is cold and your feet look like prune. There are so many small ways to find peace even for a moment and while most people (it's me, I'm most people) will tell you to focus your mind and energy towards things that help you improve yourself, I am also the person who will tell you that you need an escape hatch from the reality of life during this season. You will try to make excuses as to why you can't find peace, the kids, your job, your living situation. Nope. No excuses, you have to make it happen, even if it's only for a minute or two a day. Your ability to get through this time in your life requires you to find small ways to take care of yourself. So, get in that hot bath tub or tune in to Dax and Monica with the other Armchairies, and once you've had your moment, get right back at doing the next right thing.

Every Day After

7

KENNYISMS

My Grandpa Kenny was a quiet man filled with many things to say. If you knew him, you would have hit the lottery in life. He was special, in the "they don't make em' like they used to" kind of way. Grandpa Kenny had 9 decades worth of stories to tell and a memory as sharp as a tac. This man could tell you about what seemed like every person he ever encountered over almost a 100 year lifetime and he could do so in incredible detail, but you only heard his stories if you were really listening. He wasn't loud. He wasn't boastful. He was sharp and smart and full of sly wit. With an orneriness in his eye he would dole out hysterical one liners laced with fitting wisdom. Sometimes they were just straight to the point quips void of the humor, but always they were aptly timed, and perhaps because he was my Grandpa, I can't think of a time when they were wrong. Some were filled with information about cold weather and witches, some about the emotional state of a working girl while attending church, but there is one that you need to know and memorize during this time of your life. This Kennyism has been scorched in the back of my mind for years. Following the first of many break-ups with my ex, my Grandpa laid out a simple line "You've got to pull yourself up by your bootstraps and carry on" and promptly moved on from the conversation all together. No sense in spending any more time on the matter, you have to get yourself up and move forward, his message told me. I've held on to those words many times over the years and in many situations but more than ever when every wave of destruction came crashing to shore in the months after leaving. I can only imagine what my Grandpa would have thought about the chaos that my life had become but I do know what he would have said. Get up and get moving. You don't have the option to do nothing. You must pull yourself up by your bootstraps and carry on.

So what's required of us to actually live out carrying on in our lives? It's obviously not just that simple, you can't just say "well carry on then" and expect someone to pick up their whole life and know how to move forward.

The characteristic of strength comes up in this conversation a lot but what is strength and where is it coming from? That is a whole different book in and of itself. We are going to touch on the topic here because I think it's important to remember where we are coming from and what skills we do have to make it through this time.

In seasons such as the one you are experiencing it's common to hear words like "you're so strong" or "you're the strongest person I know" from friends and family. It can often feel blank or empty when you are in the midst of trauma to hear these words; however; there's a powerful reason for us to focus on them. Not because you need a boost from positive self talk but because you need to remember the reasons you are in fact strong. It's not about the characteristic itself, it's about the reason you have the characteristic at all. Having the ability to carry on doesn't just magically exist. You have the ability because of the scars you bear. Because of the infinite number of experiences you can recall when you were left to pick up the pieces and try as you might to put them back together, again and again. You've done this. You've carried on. Each time your partner's actions caused pain or hardship in your life, you found a way to stand up again and continue on.

This time, after you pull yourself up by the bootstraps, you will turn your boots around and walk in a different direction. This time, when you hear "you're so strong" you will use those words as a reminder of the reasons in the past you had to be strong and use them as the fuel to put one bootstrapped foot in front of the other.

Do you remember the iconic scene from the movie Beaches, when CC screams at Hillary "You're not dead yet: so stop living as if you are!" ? If you haven't seen this movie, I give you permission to put this book down immediately and run to wherever you can watch it before I ruin it for you. Oh, and fair warning, you need a box of tissues and likely a bowl of ice cream to make it through this one. Back to the point I was making, in the movie CC and Hillary are life-long friends who have led incredibly different lives but have a unique friendship that supports them through life's troubles. The quick summary is that Hillary is dying and CC is there with her and her daughter in her final days. While we know Hillary doesn't have long to be with her daughter, she begins to check out from engaging with life instead of making the most of each moment she has left. CC will have nothing of it and let's her have it with the truth "You're not dead yet: so stop living as if you are!"

What does this have to do with where you are in your life? Everything!

Are you dying? Maybe not in the sense that you will be leaving this earth soon, but your soul is in fact dying every day that you stay down in the darkness that comes with leaving your toxic partner. Some of you have made the decision to live as if you are dead. Friend, wake up! You have a life to live even if right now the days aren't perfect and they are hard, you are still alive. You have a life to live and you need to get up and start living it.

Tips to remember:

It's the little things: As you face the days following leaving your relationship behind, keep in mind that you do not have to conquer Everest in a day. Small steps forward are still steps forward and some days your wins will be bigger than others. Today it might be that you put on makeup, tomorrow it may be that you started a new bank account. The only thing that matters is that you do in fact do something. Carrying on means that you have to choose to take action that will positively support the decision you've made.

Block anyone on social media that doesn't bring joy to your life, fill out a few job applications, make an appointment with a counselor, make plans to see family or friends, start a project you've been waiting to do…there are endless things to be done so long as you choose to get up and do them.

Use your imagination: Here is one of the only passes I am going to give you on playing the what if game. In this case, I want you to take a deep dive in to the things that could happen IF you didn't choose to pull yourself out of bed every morning. Who would feel the consequences if you choose to do nothing and stay inside your hardship? What would happen to you and those around you if you simply decided to let the pain and sadness take over your life? There are only two outcomes when we go through trials, we either come out the other side a better version of ourselves or we double down on the negative and are made worse because of it. In this moment, looking at what kind of person you would be if you allowed this to destroy you, you must use this anti-version of what you want for yourself to feed your ambition to keep going.

8

BACK TO YOUR FUTURE

I want you to close your eyes, take a deep breath, and finish this sentence: in the future I will be _____.

How'd that go? If you are like I was, it might be a struggle to define what your today will look like let alone think about what the future might hold. The concept of the future seems impossible to focus our energy on when our worlds have been turned upside down. It's a struggle to even understand what is important to us, because now that everything has changed, things that once mattered simply don't anymore.

You might feel lost and unsure of where you are headed and at the same time be completely unable to decide which direction you want to go from here.

Before we dive into the ways you can envision and realize your future, we need to cover one topic that is essential to your success in this area. Without it, you will find it to be extremely difficult to navigate your path. With it you will find a place of truthful refuge when stormy days come to find you. I said in the outset of this book that I would not be using technical or clinical jargon to communicate with you, and I meant it, but this is the part where you will likely feel similarities with the wildly overused term of codependency. While I don't think we are served by placing labels on our shoulders, especially in times of crisis, I do think it's important to understand some of the unseen forces impacting our realities. So, what could ruin your ability to reimagine your future?

It's inevitable that after a period of time has passed you will either naturally or by way of other people's curiosities be asked…what now?

My friend, I stumbled hard on this one.

Every time I would start to think about what the future would hold, I found myself searching for him inside of the answer. Not in a way that said I want him in my life…trust me…not at all…but in a way that I was constantly planning my life around what chaos he would bring into it. If I started a new business, would he find out and try to sabotage my name? If I decided to move out of state would he fight me in court to try to stop me? If I started dating, would he interfere? It was even more intense when the scenarios involved our daughter. The way codependent thinking showed up for me here meant that every future plan I could dream up was tied to a scenario in which he had control or impact. It was so woven in my thought process that it wasn't a conscious decision to include him, it just happened, and I can imagine you will run up against the same factor. It took me longer than I want to admit to see that me now, and certainly not me in the future, needed to care what he thought, or felt, or cared about a damn thing I did and his reactions to those decisions were not my responsibility. If he threw a fit, that was on him. If he lashed out, that's on him. Zero plans I had for my future required me considering him in any way. Every time I allowed myself to dream and then immediately include him in that dream, I gave him power. The only way to move outside the bounds of codependent thinking in this scenario was to lay down the weight of his actions and retrain my thoughts to exclude him. I can hear you asking the obvious question…so, how'd you do it? Thought by thought.

I was driving home from a weekend trip to North Carolina when I was called out for allowing my ex's potential reaction to a decision I had made about something small, so small I don't even remember what it was now. But, I do remember the hamster wheel of thoughts that spilled out of my mouth concerning how I assumed he would react and what steps I would need to take after his impending explosion. The simple words "are you going to do this forever" were like a splash of cold water in my face. I couldn't even form the words to respond I just stared out the window watching the corn fields go by thinking:

"Of course not."

"Wait… am I?"

" Yeah."

"Probably." Said a little quieter in my head and loaded with shame.

"No!"

"HELL NO!"

And right then and there on a small town Ohio road, I made the choice to retrain my thoughts. Every time his name crept into my head in an attempt to control my decision making, I said no to myself. I stood up to myself over and over again until the hand cuffs were loosened and then finally unlocked, and my thoughts were no longer tied to him. He had no impact on my decision making because each time my mind jumped to "what if he" I simply said, no Renee.

I'd like to say that was the only stumbling block I had when I began to think forward….but that would be a lie.

Detaching from the idea that your future is intrinsically tied to the version of you that existed inside of your past is critical. In the year that followed leaving my marriage and my business, I continually came face to face with these questions "What do I do now?" and its twin "Who am I if I'm not Renee, owner of an event company?" I wrestled with these and versions of them every time I would try to focus on the future, and the truth is I still come up against them from time to time.

I'll admit, it was much easier to see myself outside of my marriage than outside of my profession. At the point where it all fell apart, I hadn't truly been his wife in years…but me as a professional, that was a different story. I was at the top of the game when it came crashing down. At the time, it seemed impossible to look five or ten years in the future and not see events. Not see myself on stage speaking at conferences. Not see myself accepting awards. Not seeing myself teaching classes. Not being the boss. I realize how gross that sounds.

For more than a decade I was Renee, the event professional. Period. In my mind the public dumpster fire that was the ending to it all meant I could no longer go back, but if I wasn't that then what the hell was I?

I couldn't see it.

I couldn't see myself as anything but that version of me.

I couldn't see it until I had no choice. It was time to find a job.

When I told my parents to take my daughter from the house the night of the accident, I put one of my only stakes in the ground. "I'll do whatever it takes to protect her." And I meant it, or so I thought. Protection can look like many things but in the season that followed the business closing that meant I had to figure out how to financially protect her. If events weren't a thing any more, then what on earth was I going to do? Had I said "I'll work at Starbucks if I have to." Yep, I sure did. And hey, those drink discounts and free Spotify account sounded like perks I could use at the time, but had I really meant I'd swap CEO for Barista? Eeehhh…maybe not. I'm grateful I had other options present themselves; however; the point of the matter is, I was scared shitless to no longer be the person I once was and I had no clue what I could be in the future if it wasn't that. I can safely assume you may face the same.

The first time I opened my computer to search for a new job I sat staring at my computer screen for an hour, bouncing between the places I previously went to to post open jobs and a dozen or so other open tabs filled with my social media accounts, random google searches, and the constant monitoring of Mycase for new updates.

I gave up after that hour. "What do I even type in the search bar?" "Anything event is out so, ummmm now what?" Close laptop. I didn't go back on the hunt for days.

Before I could think about the future, I had to see myself without my past. Purely me. No titles. No clout. No reputation, be it good or now tarnished. Just me. Doing so was a process, it's still a process. In moments where the question of what I was going to do popped up and I would start to squirm with anxiety, I shifted my questions entirely. Instead of "what now?" I began to ask "what matters?". It was time to call my own bullshit.

It took realizing that this was a tangled mess of ego colliding with limiting beliefs about who I truly was and what I was actually capable of to pull my future into focus. I had come to this idea of planning my future holding onto the Renee I thought I had to keep up with. I was embarrassed and worried that any career move I made would become one more thing to talk about and somehow would mean that I was less than. That last part. Less than. Oooh that's a prickly little sucker.

There it was, the thing holding me back. In my attempt to look forward at what could be, I allowed my future self to be codependent with my past self. I needed her in order to feel worthy. I couldn't exist without her. Could I?Bit by bit, I examined myself and what it meant to be me and bit by bit I removed the associations to my past. It took removing my ego to see I was much more than my career highlights. Stripped of all the things I thought defined me, I learned to see the skills, and more importantly the mindset, that had gotten me this far could carry me anywhere I wanted to go. Planning from a place of wide open possibility meant I could dream bigger than I previously allowed myself to and the evidence of the success in my past meant I had the proven ability to do it again. All I had to do was go for it.

In the moments where you are faced with the inevitable talk of your future, I want you to remember these two truths: you are not shackled to "what if they" thinking and the things that previously defined you are completely changeable. As you move through this process there will likely be occasions where you are frozen in a place of uncertainty or worse, you will find yourself doom spiraling. Look, we said we were going to be truthful with one another, and it's bound to happen so I'm here to prepare you. As you bump up against these times, I want you to take 2 minutes to just breathe. Literally. Focus on nothing but your breathing, and bonus if you can literally stand up right where you are and… just…

breath. In. And out. In. And out. And then I want you to ask yourself one question: "what matters." Let the answer guide you. Let the answer become your path forward. As it evolves, adjust your course accordingly. Allowing what matters and the simplicity of those things to be your center will shine a light on the things you include as you plan your future.

When the world is ugly and you face the questions of others or your own, come back to this grounding. Breathe. What matters?

Tips to remember:

Tomorrow will come: How many nights have you kept yourself awake because you didn't know how to face the next day? Friend. We've ALL been there but the thing about it is, tomorrow's gonna come so you might as well have a plan in place to tackle that SOB. Planning is essential to peace. As you come through this season of your life, this may start slowly. Plan a few days at a time, then a week, then a month. You get it. Start small with things like meal planning and putting blocks of time on your phone calendar for must do and want to do tasks.

Once you've established some of these, start to stack more of them and over time you will find peace knowing things are laid out in front of you, that there is certainty in your day that you can rely on. Your future starts at this moment, right now as you are reading these words.

Shadows: Do you remember Peter Pan, yeah we are talking about him again, and how his shadow was always toying with him? Yours will too. As you navigate the waters of moving forward in your life there will be times when you and your shadow self will dance. It's up to you to decide if that's a beautiful tango or a fight to the death dance off. The point is, you will come face to face with situations where you see yourself now and the shadowed version of yourself that existed in your past. Embrace both but keep your eyes on who you are today not on who you were previously. You will need to decide what parts of your shadow are worthy of chasing after to reattach and which ones you'd rather not bring back to Neverland.

Decisions Have A Return Policy: This should come as no surprise, but everything in your life can be changed. Up until now we've largely discussed this concept with sensitive regard to what we've lost in our lives but, there's good news in this concept if you choose to look for it. Here is one of the best silver linings I can give you: your decisions about your future can be changed. Yep. It's that simple. You can make a decision today that you are going to go back to school, work three jobs to save money, take a sabbatical to work on you and you alone, move to the other side of the world, change your name, literally anything and at any given time beyond this moment you can return to that decision and change your mind. Embrace the freedom that comes with owning your decisions. You can, will, and should evaluate your decisions often and adjust course as needed. Let the true barometer of "what matters" guide you.

9

I AM THE PARENT

Hey momma, I see you.

I see you wondering how you are going to make it. I see you praying every night that you are strong enough for them. I see you crying in the bathtub so she doesn't know how hard of a day it's been. Momma. I see you and I need you to know that means you aren't alone.

Parenting in this season of your life is not pretty. It's not social media worthy. It's not matching pjs at Christmas or play dates while the moms sip lattes. These days look like attending Dads with donuts day because he isn't allowed on school property and you are one of three women sitting at primary colored little people lunch tables not touching a bite of that delicious Amish Crack Donut. (If you know, you know. If you don't immediately find out.)

This is probably one of the hardest things for me to talk about. Every fiber of my being wants to hide it away and not look at the ugly mistakes I've made parenting my daughter. And yet it's a conversation that is essential. I could write an entire book about this topic alone. I'll say this as a matter of honesty: some of this is going to be do as I say not as I do. BUT....the truth is still the truth. They say "nothing prepares you for motherhood" and while that can't be argued, let's double down and say "nothing prepares you for parenting a child who has experienced trauma." Please keep in mind there is no rule book here. No one person has this completely figured out. The best we can do is break down some fundamentals that will help you navigate these choppy waters. And pray.

I've come to terms with the understanding that I will go to my grave with regrets from my daughter's childhood. The amount of time I lost, that *we* lost, together and the things she didn't get from me that she undoubtedly needed will gnaw away at me for my lifetime. Often inside of relationships like those we've experienced, decisions are made with frail mindsets and raw emotion leaving all kinds of room for things we would take back if we could. This is especially true with regards to parenting inside an abusive relationship.

That fact does not; however; erase or excuse the damage those decisions cause and while we cannot change the past, we can address the present and future impact those decisions will have on both our children and ourselves.

It was a particularly rough morning, 30 minutes of shouting and a wall of ticking clocks telling me it was nearing time to leave for the more than hour long round trip drive to school drop off and back. We rushed off to the car with more attitude than any morning can handle. Both exhausted, drained, and both just at our limit. We pulled out of the driveway and I was yelling, not in a gentle yet firm way, I was full on rage yelling. "You have to listen to me." "You cannot be disrespectful." "You need to get up and get ready when I say so." "You will not treat me like he did." Ouch. By the time we made it to the highway, which is less than 2 minutes from the house, we were both silent. Sitting there staring at a red light in the dark stillness that the early morning brings, I looked over at her, seeing tears streaming down her little face, and I apologized. It hit me like a cold glass of water tossed over your head, all the moments over her short little lifetime that I had failed her and now inside the hardest days of her life, I had never once truly apologized for what she was having to go through.

It wasn't her fault. It wasn't something she should have to carry. Who the hell was I to be mad that this little girl let her emotions spill over the top of her glass because she was tired in every sense of the word, confused, and completely scared? How could I take my own emotional mess and let it show up in early morning frustrations? How could I ever elude to comparing her to him. Well…I did, and I'd wager that you also have or will have a time or two. In that very moment, on that cold morning, I could see so clearly that this was in fact not about being late to school or not listening when told to do something, it was about us both being broken and scared and she needed me to step up and be her parent. She needed me to be the example. The apology wasn't perfect but it did let her know that I recognized she had been wronged time and time again and that she deserved more, out of both of us. That it was okay to be sad, and mad, and scared, and confused. That what she had experienced was wrong and shouldn't have happened to her. That she was worthy of better and owed an apology. Fifteen minutes later we were singing Disney songs. For the record, we also made it to school on time.

I am a firm believer that kids who go through trauma should be talked to in an adult manner. Are they adults? No. Should they be told everything?

Also no. But, they have seen and heard some of the worst adult things and pretending as if they haven't isn't helpful to anyone. I also believe, not every child is the same and this approach may not work for everyone. In my case, I chose to approach my daughter with two things in mind: she needs the tools to navigate her emotions and develop her mindset, and she needs to know she is still a child so it's okay to act like one as long as she is respectful.

Talking with my daughter will be one of the most rewarding things I hold on to from this time in our lives. The drives too and from school, rehearsals, and friend's houses were filled with raw conversations about how we can grow from darkness into light. Those moments are etched in my mind. From them came healing. From them came understanding of both her journey and my own. From them came new discoveries of abuse. This time brought me more insight than any other time we spent together. Slowly she shared more and more about her own story. She spoke of the things she had gone through, memories she had, and the anger she had built up inside her. There was so much I didn't know. At first, her instinct to protect her father was strong and the pain of losing her home and possessions was too much for her to hold on her own.

Much of our early discussions were laced with vicious accusations and fierce defense but as I listened and questioned, she softened. It was obvious she needed someone to be the punching bag and momma...let me give you a warning, it's going to be you. It's going to be you that gets the front car on the ugly roller coaster of your child's emotional roller coaster. The ups and downs, twists and turns, it's you that will have to stand strong through it all for them, especially through the stomach turning curves. You are likely to face moments where blame is laid at your feet and moments where they will blame themselves. Moments where they cling to happy memories and times when they recall memories that you know aren't exactly true. That was one of the hardest parts of the journey I had to navigate. In my efforts to encourage her to talk I was faced with times when the story she was telling wasn't entirely accurate and I questioned if I had it in me to defend him or to make sure she knew he loved her. This was a test we will all face at some point or another inside parenting through trauma; can you put yourself last? It wasn't about me, it can't ever be about me. The cardinal rule I learned in this season was no matter what truth had to lead because it would always be what was best for her and sometimes that truth was she wasn't always the victim and he wasn't always the scary monster under the bed and I was the one that had to hold the truth in the light.the one that had to hold the truth in the light.

"She doesn't trust you to be the parent." On a Tuesday morning while sitting in a therapy session with my daughter, these words forced me to come face to face with the parent I thought I was, and the one I really had been up to that point. "Excuse me, who the hell do you think you are?" I said. Just kidding…but it is what I thought until I snapped back to reality and sitting there in a dimly lit rental office, I realized she was absolutely right. My actions, or inactions in many cases, had established a pattern that my daughter recognized as a time when she had to be self reliant. Either physically or emotionally. Whether that came during times when I was out of town for work and she ate candy for breakfast that she had hidden in her room so she'd have something to eat, or when I could only sit on the top step of our stairs frozen physically and mentally while she played alone in her toy room next to me…there were more times than I can count in her short years on this planet that she felt she needed to care for herself in one way or another. And now that I had my shit (mostly) together, well what did that change for her? Turns out, nothing. She was stuck inside a life we no longer lived and I had failed to see I needed to start from ground zero with her if we were ever going to get out together. The most valuable information I learned in this season with her is that she needed boundaries just as much as she needed grace. The softness I showed towards her because she had been through so much was both a blessing and a curse. I had allowed both of us to sit in grief for too long without proving to her that I was the parent she had needed since her first breath all the way to today. When emotions overflowed I had allowed the excuses to flow right along with them. In that moment, sitting in an oversized chair, looking at coloring pages laid out for kiddos to use during their therapy sessions, I shifted my thinking entirely. Instead of trying to de-escalate when she lashed out at me, I met her with a firm stance. We are not victims and we will not be disrespectful. We can feel what we feel, but we are not allowed to use emotions as weapons on others or ourselves. We will not stay stuck. And one of the most painful realizations: we will not allow our relationship to mirror the one she witnessed. Boundaries became our focus. In many ways it felt like I was working through areas I hadn't addressed with her father. Setting expectations for what I would and wouldn't tolerate wasn't easy nor did it come quickly but it was exactly what we both needed. She knew I was her provider but she needed to know I was also her guard rail.

The conversation in therapy that day was the wake up I needed. "I am the parent." I say this to myself daily and to her when correction is needed. I say it not because I'm desperate for authority or control, but because my child, and every other child on the planet, needs someone to be their guard rail. We teach our toddlers right from wrong, how to share, to avoid danger, and respect others. And then they watch us. More often than not, the kids who have come through the trauma of toxic marriages see examples daily of the exact opposite. I owed it to her to show her examples of how it should have been done her whole life. I owed it to her to have conversation after conversation explaining why all the sudden it felt like I changed…because I did. She needed to know, I made mistakes and I recognized those but that no longer were we going to allow each other to sit inside something that wasn't helping us grow. And most importantly, we both needed to know, the boundaries of respect and discipline were real. This meant when she bumped up against a guard rail, I was there to send her back to center and I had to do it every…single…time. Not sometimes. Not occasionally. Not on days when I was feeling strong and whole. No. Everytime. And yes, she hated it. It also meant I had to clearly call out her ability to manipulate the situation with her emotions.

And look, let's be real a second, when a momma (especially a wounded one) sees her child express sadness and angst we rush to make things better. It is our immediate instinctual reaction...and my friend, they know it. Yes! Our children know that the second things are getting a bit tight they can tip the table by bringing out the residual emotions of their trauma and boom, the focus is now off of discipline and on to empathy. Hear me when I say this, you can and will need to hold both discipline AND empathy in the moment. When I saw her defense walls starting to go up, I began to recognize that we were about to enter the victimizing mindset spiral we had been stuck in. The only way out was through, if you haven't recognized yet, it's a common theme. We had to sit together and look straight at what was going on, call a spade a spade, and I had to draw the line in the sand. No longer were we using a backlog of emotions to manipulate the present. Every day from then forward we relied on that foundation to reestablish the dynamic of our relationship and the consistent reliability she now saw in my responses brought the trust we both needed.

I won't sugar coat this. It's a process and it is not going to be a fun one. Sometimes you will feel like you are on a hamster wheel going 1mph to nowhere. I can also assure you that you MUST take the role of parenting your child. Did we not say we wanted more for our children? Did we not say we wanted something better? Then give it to them. You can no longer allow them to view you as an optional participant. You can longer allow them to rely on themselves for their emotional and mental well being. YOU are the parent!

Tips to remember:

They aren't them: I was on a call coming home from school drop off and chatting with a friend of mine. It was a normal "how are things" check up call not too long after my world imploded and I was venting about seeing behaviors in my daughter that reminded me of him. The sharp tongue, disrespect, emotional swings. I was scared. Mostly I was mad. Mad that she had learned that it was okay to treat me that way. Mad that I let it happen. Mad that there was even an ounce of his negative characteristics showing up in MY daughter. Ew. God bless my friend. The warning wasn't what I wanted to hear but it was straight to the point. "Never compare her to him." In her own life she had been through an experience when she was young that was not too far off from ours and gave sound advice that it would do no good and in fact serious harm to my daughter to ever hear words comparing her to her father in a negative way. Did I get it right from there on? No. But I have learned, listened, and apologized for making this misstep and hope you hear this as loud as it takes to keep you from doing the same. They are not them.

Find A Guide: I cannot stress this enough, you are going to need help. Seeking professional help for my daughter was one of the best parenting decisions I've ever made. I knew early on that I was out of my league with this one and not only was I so deep in my own healing that I couldn't be all she needed, the real truth is, she needed it to not be me. She needed a neutral source of support. Someone who didn't know me, didn't know her father, and didn't have predetermined feelings or thoughts about the situation. The first stages for us looked very light and focused mostly on general feelings. As we progressed it was evident we needed something more to bring out deeper healing from things we didn't even know were things at the time. While I can't tell you what will work best for you or your child, I can tell you that leaning into professional support was the single most valuable tool we found along our journey. You will know what works for you. If you don't find it with your first resource, keep looking. Keep advocating. The healing done here will strengthen you and your child as individuals and as a team.

"I'm not a baby anymore!" : There's simply no denying that kids who have gone through it at home grow up faster than they should. It's equally as true that they are often less mature than their peers. So what do we do with tiny humans who have emotional maturity shortcomings and adult experiences? Meet them right where they are. From day to day and sometimes minute to minute, we need to meet our kids where they are while acknowledging they are allowed to be children. As I focused more and more on my daughter during times where her cup was overflowing, I found that she was stuck at an emotional maturity plateau. She was showing me behavior typical for the age several years younger than she was and as I started to thread together similarities, it clicked. She was stuck at the emotional age of when she began witnessing the toxicity of her parents' marriage and while she was desperate to be seen as grown up, in her most vulnerable moments that little scared girl showed up time and time again. Instead of being frustrated with her for seeming to revert backwards every time things got tough, I recognized she needed me to help her move forward. Unpacking the memories, both good and bad, seeing them for what they really were, and leaving them in a safe place in her mind allowed her the freedom to move on and grow.

10
MOVING ON

If you would have told me when I first opened the file to start writing this book that I would be finishing it ready to get married again, I would have told you to immediately check yourself into a psych ward. What?! I can safely say, I did not see this coming. As I type, the man that showed me that my life was worth reclaiming is sitting in front of me playing video games after a normal day of normal living. Going to work. Making dinner. Doing the dishes…together. Okay I know that's not normal but hey, I got really lucky with this one.

I've thought long and hard about how to close this out. There is so much I want you to know and yet, I feel like I've said it all except this: You can and will move on. I know at this moment it may not feel like it, and heck, I won't even encourage you to until the time is right, but there will come a day when you wake up and there will be a thought that creeps into your mind and you will know, it's time to lay it all down and move on. On from the hurt. On from the pain. On from the stuckness of it all. And while it doesn't have to look like a new relationship, one day, just like that, you will be ready to reclaim your life.

Last year my uncle passed away. He was as ornery as they come and his last days were filled with moments that our family will talk about for ages. One of those my cousin shared with me recently. It was a simple statement "Get Renee to wear color." Eye roll. I love my black clothes. The day of his funeral was as to be expected. That side of my family is close. We spent the day in mourning together and all the while, my phone was buzzing. I spent the entire day talking to a man I had met online a few days prior. I hadn't felt that rush of joy in almost two decades. A few short weeks later I was out Christmas shopping with my Aunt, my Uncle's wife, and while I'm not really sure how the conversation went, the result was I walked out of the store with a new gray sweater. Looking back now, I chuckle a bit that gray was a big step forward for me. It took me six more months to shed the all black, all day, every day clothing, but the connection can't be overlooked. The man I had just met turned out to be the path to getting "Renee to wear color." Not because I can't rock the all black, I totally can, but because he showed me that I was hiding myself behind a shield of clothing. Through conversations and introspection, I realized that I had created a persona to shield myself from the world because I had lost my self-esteem in my previous relationship. I had hidden behind an image that no longer served me, and I couldn't recognize the person I had become. Slowly I found myself emerging, the physical transformation looking back at it now is truly unbelievable. I see the black clothes silver haired version of me and wonder how on earth I looked at myself in the mirror and didn't see it for what it was. What I know seems so surface level, was a complete awakening of who I really am as a person. I had been hiding behind an image that I can't even recognize anymore. Who the heck was that girl? It was time to shed that old self and embrace the real me, in whatever colors I chose.

  I was equal parts ready and completely unprepared to move on in my life. I ventured into a new job, completely different from the industry I had known for years. I committed to taking care of my physical and emotional well-being, focusing on looking and feeling my best. And, of course, I embarked on a new relationship, which was a daunting prospect after my tumultuous marriage.

It sounds so easy. So normal. And yet, I had no idea how to handle it all. The idea of dating seemed ridiculous. How does that work in your 40's? Do you just blurt out all the awful things you've been through in your previous relationships and hope you don't scare the crap out of the person on the other end of whatever app you've chosen as your matchmaker? Yikes. I was clueless. But, I dipped my toe in the water anyway. What started as a daily text to my best friend with screenshots of the funniest profile photos I had come across came to a day when I stopped dead in my tracks with a return message from a guy who would turn out to be my future. I was terrified. Don't screw it up Renee.

I'll spare you the teenage love story and skip to the part that will serve as a warning for you. You will bump up against your past, often. It was, and still is a year later, an ongoing battle to not bleed old blood all over what is new. specially when it's impossible to be completely severed from your past.

It isn't a conscious choice to bring your damaged heart into a new relationship, and you'll try everything not to, but the reality is that broken bitch follows you and makes herself known at the most random times. It may be in a comparison, maybe it will be oversharing of stories, or maybe you will struggle with healthy relationship traits. One thing I can safely guarantee you is that at some point if you choose to enter into a new relationship your new partner will feel the impact of your brokenness. Inside of these moments, communication will be your saving grace. When you recognize that you're bringing your past into your present, it's crucial to address it openly and honestly with your partner. I had to make a choice: continue to be stuck in dysfunctional patterns or acknowledge that I needed to grow and heal. It wasn't easy, but it was necessary for the health of my new relationship.

Learning how to love and be loved again is a precarious thing. Just the thought of being hurt again is enough to keep most of us from even considering it. But here I am, a year later, sitting with the man who has shown me that love can be different. It can be kind, patient, and nurturing. It can be a source of healing rather than pain.

And while I can't promise that it will be smooth sailing for everyone, I can say this: it is possible to move on from the hurt and pain of the past. The journey of healing and finding love again is not without its challenges. It's a process of rediscovering yourself and shedding the layers of protection you've built up over the years. For me, it started with something as simple as wearing color instead of sticking to my usual all-black attire. It may seem trivial, but it was a symbolic step towards embracing my true self. Truly opening yourself up to love again is a delicate journey. The fear of being hurt once more can be paralyzing, but it's a risk worth taking. It's a process of growth, healing, and rediscovery. And while I can't guarantee that it will be without its ups and downs, I can say that it is possible to move on, find love, and experience a relationship that brings joy, healing, and happiness into your life.

To anyone who may be in a similar place as I was when I began this journey, I offer this message of hope: You can and will move on. You can reclaim your life, find peace, and if you choose to… love again. It is likely to take time, effort, and a lot of self-reflection, but I am living breathing proof that it is possible.

And when you do, you'll discover that as painful as what you've been through can be, the other side of this journey can be a beautiful, transformative force that brings light to even the darkest days.

xoxoxo,

Renee

Tips to remember:

Vulnerability: Whew, deep breath! That's a scary word huh? While it's important to be open and vulnerable in a new relationship, it's equally important to take things at a pace that feels right for you. Don't feel pressured to rush into sharing your deepest emotions or experiences too quickly. You will know what feels right for you. Allow trust to develop on its own. Guard your heart, your boundaries, and your wounds carefully but do so in a way that leaves room for someone to enter.

It's Your Life: Queue Bon Jovi, a tan Honda Accord, and Daytona Beach, it's anthem time. Look, it's your life we are talking about here and as we've covered about 734 times before in this book, you get to call the shots. If you are ready to move on in your life, that's your call. No one else's. Literally no one. Not your momma, not your bestie, not your kid, not your therapist…yours. You will know when that time comes. Listen to yourself. If you feel ready, then prepare yourself and venture out into the world.

They Are Not Them: If I could get you to hear one thing about getting into a new relationship it would be this: they are NOT them. All the painful, terrible moments you've experienced in the past will lie to you as you enter a new relationship. You will search for reasons this new person is like your ex, you will dig for reasons to not trust them, you will guard your heart like this person was a vampire ready to suck you dry. Hey. HEY! Listen. This human who you've connected with and who has expressed care and interest for you, is not your past. When doubt creeps in or you find yourself dragging your baggage along on a date, remind yourself that you don't live that life anymore, and they are not them.

www.ingramcontent.com/pod-product-compliance
Lightning Source LLC
Chambersburg PA
CBHW070202100426
42743CB00013B/3023